Battered Soul

FRANK KARAN

Matchstick Literary
1-888-306-8885
orders@matchliterary.com

ACQUIRE YOUR TOKEN

All away from home Tim out here on my own
My aging muscles are far from been toned
Like a magnificent warrior who has been disowned
Emphatically recalling the bloody mighty battles

My mind is abating; the emotions keep debating
Our limbicallabour is akin to dwarfing vapour
Flitting in a vagrant laugh bickering at staff
Your trying to hold your composure but there's

Some hidden clause highlighting the pitfalls
Of exposure; with such minimal disclosure
It's time for you to acquire your token
Because the universe has calmly spoken

ANIMISTIC SUBCULTURE

You're so opinionated that you've always got
Something to say gratuitously emanating from
Your puritanical smile, as you lamely stagger
Like some gaudy madden office clerk garnishly

Beguiling his tortoiseshell intolerable computer hooks
Intercedingly speaking in a domesticated commentary of
Unperturbed expletives from a glumly respirable little
Podgy man; within a micro archaic animistic subculture

The plutocracy of the typically fantasied aficionado
Miffs a rectitude of unintelligible tastily abandoned
Off beat distinguished intoning. How negligent is the
Purse gunning deceit? So where is your valid receipt?

ARID TALK

My voice sounded like a rusted carburetor
As my heart sunk a thousand fathoms down
The slim line between momentary madness
And eternal sadness, vividly mocked my
Sense of self worth regressing me into

Still birth! The loneliness gulped my
Steadfast throat, wrenching it like a
Worn out throttle; my mouth was fuming like
A punctured exhaust, starving the flakiness
Of superficial monotonous sulking arid talk

AQUA HUE

A tantalising aqua hue is beaming off the waning
Crescent moon, freshening the cinematic nightsky
Accomodating it's wavering ecliptic light like
Some alien lifeforce, surging towards humanity

My face turns watermelon red and my mind is all
Numbing dead; in a blotchy insular sump I dread
You're constantly blocking objections n'intolerably
Annuling exemptions, what about all the rejections?

BATTERED SOUL

Only my battered soul knows how it survived
Hurrying thru the perilous jungle mountains
Of India, Pakistan and Nepal into enfiliading
Chinese eyes, only I know what I've been thru

And why; there were monstrous foot soldiers
Chasing 'provoking me but none came to see
What temptations did the demons throw at me
Humiliating anguish and armoured aggression

Were bestowed on me; exhuming any breath that
Remained in my etiolated body. In my quest to
Be pure I had to endure! The righteous life
Endeavoured to live kept all the wretchedness

Away; the broken windows of your soul, reveal
The glory that you've sold, the goodness that
Once was envied n 'pristine holds little esteem
Words that are hastily spoken are often broken

There's a remainder embedded in your cry as
Your body loses it's will to survive with a
Ghostly light appeasing the tendrill of life
It's burdening in 'crippling rife, causing the

Tranquil lullness encrypting our missionary
Plight; the visionary notion of freeing holy
My battered soul empowers me to attain my goal
So I can banish injustice and tyranny in whole

FLICOSE BEREAVEMENTS

You yell like a damsel in distress, as you
Fall off the stage in a mess, the emotions
Keep independently racing as I mutterly do
Confess, overlapping is the harpsichord of

You're innocent soul, lying in an aridly
Dry constituent zone, a self calculating
Intimacy lies coherent; readily grasping
The imperceptible heightened concealment

Embellishing the hallmarks of a secular
Permanency of achievement, hypnotically
Transfixed, mostly in lasciviously wild
Forms of bizzare, belicose bereavements

BETTER BUFF

You're such a loving sensation which I can't deny
All I ever wish for you is to gracefully fly high
Whilst picknicking in the swamp you incite a romp
Trumpling thru a narrowing cove, turning the rove

When the windblown gate shifts thru the prism wurley
I hesitantly venture into a cosmic horizon too early
My imagination keeps shivering in the hot gloomy dusk
Your brim braced isometric cap shines like ivory tusk

My emotions are running out of puff as I put on my shiny
Prismatic golden cuff, denouncing me from à vagrant duff
Making me feel highly prized like rejuvenated clever stuff
Likewise I'm shaking off the deadwood to get a better buff

BITTER ENEMIES

I'm slowly melting like a waning candle
After you nailed me to the wooden cross
Why do you violate our ancestoral ways?
Obscuring nonsecular simple tribal ways

You don't have to send your camels to bed
Just imagine; the problems in you're head
There's no such thing as an untouchable heart
But you prounce around, with a watchdog chart

We must dig up all the dirty, muddy trenches
To reduce the bitter enemies waring defences
Can you feel the freedom, lingering in the air?
And the love that's always free for us to share

BOLSTERING MY CREED

To the flapping feathers of birds in flight
Observing the frivolent fish swimming tight
Wghilst gazing at the multitude of amazingly
Fresh greenery, bursting in brilliant light

The ambient features of sparkling colourful flowers
And the scent of wonderful aromas do reach the moon
Skipping through potholes of blossoming roses n'tulips
I felt recharged and priggishly marred without a doubt

I curiously pondered what all the fuss was justifiably about
Watching rodent rabbits and hares running into their burrows
Luxuriating they're breed, in turn I straddled bolstering my
    creed
Suddenly T stopped to think. why does the world have so
    much greed?

CALLOUS BEAT

Why don't I feel the same way that i used to feel?
Can you revive me with your tantalising love pill?
Your always testing me by examining my love for you
Emotionally you're just too weak, to reach the peak

I carefully listen to the pitter patter of your feet
And the weeping weening sounds, of your callous beat
Your eyes look distantly cold as you forfeited the fold
Do we have to wait till we're old to clutch at the gold

BECOME A PAIR

You have to have a fast furious pace
Just to be in the Grand Prix race
Where there is no sorry disqrace
Just actual accelerated mace

Though your eyes smile so bright
And make me feel, tenderly right
They disintegrate all of my lies

Then cut me down to slender size
All I really wanted was you
To stick by me and be true
Think of what we share When we unite, become a pair

CATCH THE RAINBOW

You can catch the rainbow in your hand
You can make a ship sail onto dry land
You can pull the thunder out of the sky
You can turn the darkest night into day

An burrow beneath the sordid clay
Which dangerous sport do you play
What else have you got to openly say
Surely there "S a place you must pray

Love is available on a single silver tray
And beckons in a strange exhilirating way
You can whisk you're troubles so far away
Then sift unaccentedly thru the lofty hay

CATHEXIS

I want to reach out and touch the love in your eyes
They're like a lonesome star which perfectly shines
They brighten us up with an aura of heavenly light
Closetting a velvety curtain from clannish delight

You're words are of happiness, gentle and serene
I feel such a radiant warmth that's ever so keen
I never could imaqine you been so horribly mean
How can we solve all of our problems in between

We learn to paint the classicize portrait of ourselves
Our cathexis displays a varied range of tender emotion
Snugly ensconed in an ambulatory apse, mildly entraining
Those ambiverted characteristics; wedged in you're lapse

CELESTIAL FRUIT

You jolt so hurriedly like
A rabbit facing headlights
Bopping in silvery shadows
Treading in calfskin boots

Quintessentially fetching celestial
Fruit, misapprehending a marvellous
Connectedness, nattering it's false
Optimism of radiant moonstruck love

You're olive green zephr eyes expose
an eternal warmth 'cyclical mystery
Laddened in a golden fabulousness of
Almighty determination 'abomination

CLEANSE YOUR SOUL

Leave all of your troubling doubts behind
Far distant in yesterday's, horizon's eye
Cleanse your soul of despair and sad fate
Think of yourself as man's pure soul mate

I do enjoy the calmness of you're breath
And the subtle stillness of you're depth
You must watch where you carefully step
Your like the shepherd that hates sheep

But angrily growls at the wolf's teeth
Your not irreparable; so why not sleep?
Is that a thought that's less than cheap
Is there a silence, which you must keep?

CLASSIC AMBIENCE

I'm gazing at the earthly swaying mood and at
The colours of the clouds 'the slewing froth
From the pulsating fluffy surf, the baldingly
Airy light is intently regulated 'circumvented
In a cool aesthetic compliance evoking timeless

Classic ambience hankered by a serviceable style
I'm so happily infatuated with you're glittering
Smile which rejuvenates me once in a sweet while
Your delectable fantasies are dodging with rejection
How extensively lucrative are your secret intentions

CLEMENT STYLE

A hungry lion kills with royal nobility
And ferocious agility, there's no shame
Or fear even if you instantly disappear
The present is escaping, from it's past

Peering at the deadly crevice downcast
You always look great, dressed in navy
Dark blue, and my love for you is true
I wanted to play you like a didgeridoo

So please lend me your pedimanous hand
We'll drink then excitedly eat the jam
It's time to let the magic genie, out of
The ancient bottle 'rev up the throttle

You're dingily distinct, but not extinct
Be content with life disregard the tripe
You're clement style topples the gridlock
Mile, then you soothe with a hasten smile

CLIMACTERIC

You pomply run fast over creaky single lane
Wooden bridges to see the sandy blue beaches
It's a clampdown of climacteric episodes in
You're perplexing vainglorious stringed life

There's an unsettling wind breezing vastly
Over our rain drenched soggy wet cold heads
Why do you mainly give nice burnt offerings
When you don't receive any single openings

You're jet lagged emotions are lazily causing a
Temporary heartache. erupting like an earthquake
In a semi detached vernacular state of shock,
I Had a mental block! Can you take off your frock?

COCONUT RUM

We can lose ourselves on a steaming hot tropical isle
And seek adventure in a careless balmy paradise style
We'll leave the monotony of the civil automation mile
Relaxing in the green lagoon instead of a dark saloon

We don't need to worry about future space aeronautics
Or the circulation of white blood cells 'antibiotics
An the intricate principles of jet turbine hydraulics
All we need is to stop nagging an enjoy some real fun

Whilst surfing on the waves, giggling at the happy raves
We can explore the rock paintings in the limestone caves
Were drinking coconut rum splashing our love to everyone
Life becomes so fresh and young when we revel at the fun

CONNIVING DISASTER

You're purple powdered lips are ladened with a devilish kiss
You're eyes reflect the hidden caves, of anguishing thoughts
There's an enduring tendency to cognizantly dispel the sweet
Syrupy codswalop with a breathtaking novelty; anecdotally we

Do perceive rather astonishingly a kaleidoscopic provocative
Variety, parachuting. downwards within a sheltered harbour sea
Necessitating and recirculating the absentia agenda concealed
In the unappealing composure of your triumphantly unperturbed

Impervious blowtorched, wretched mushy gaggling nemesis drain
You're life has been littered in vain and unaccustomed strain
Your funny outbursts of laughter conceal a conniving disaster
We need to remove the querilla warfare master to build faster

CONTIGUOUS CONTEMPT

Perspicaciously i try to unfathom
Your petulant attitude towards me
Undeniably irritating is it's coldness
Personifying the feu-de-joie in you're

Ham fisted brain; shuffle boarding with
Benign skulduggery, wheedling blackmail
And utter betrayal, whilst blathering on
The inconsistency of contiguous contempt

Is there a way to voice your discontent
Obstreperous is you're man made dissent
There are nO calm breezes on rough seas
An the world around you makes you tease

CRIPPLING LONELINESS

You'rehalf baked solutions are no more than
Smutty elicit illusions, your contravening a
Not so conventional attitude variably intent
On wreaking havoc in thorny gridlocked lives

You honestly declare love when consternating
Like a balmy desert night, revealing all the
Crippling loneliness in the abstract openess
Of a dark blue summer's nightsky embodied on

Flickering shiny stars that keep teasing the
Banana shaped moon whilst wryly appeasing my
Vacant cocoon; I cannot think clearly in my room
Therefore I must return to diligently study soon

CYNICAL DESIRE

Hurriedly you slipped past me as I wanted to indulge in
A long passionate kiss, my heart was aiming not to miss
You're senses were pulsating as my mind was fornicating
Throwing me into a cynical desire, protruding me with a

Sophisticated spire, we were unable to douce the hot fire
Realistically we couldn't get any higher; you're alluring
Smile accentuates like cool clear opal waters, your heavy
Scented perfume opens up many key chained padlocked doors

With a tenacious grip, i crawled back from the unthinkable trip
Very uncertain demographics circumnavigated the unsinkable
    ship
Nervously you flick a match but you're unable to snatch or hatch
Quite lingering is the scratch, so where's you're perfect match?

DECOLLETAGE

Your decolletage appears so inviting
It lullifies my senses then pacifies
All defences; your sybaritic fumbling
Charm is chauffeur driven, by one arm

Now is not the time to raise the alarm, an
You're not all that your crunched up to be
So be careful you don't fall off the shaky
Tree. but me, I'm just living in purgatory

DEBUNKING RASH

I don't want another lecture in reverse psychology
Or some painstaking analysis of adverse pathology
I'm not an excitingly monumental piece of work
But I can always bounce back with a clean jerk

My gruelling lifestyle is highly combustible
It's not smooth sailing or sheer flusterable
If there is less for you, than meets the eye
Then I suggest that you give it one more try

Before the active world leaves you enervatingly dry
Don't expect too much; or you'll disappointedly die
If your not ostentatiously brash, then don't dogodaedaly crash
The disanimating nostology of life is akin to a debunking rash

DUSTBIN OF YOUR LIFE

Tossing in the whirlpool of your brain
Is a ghastly writhing shudder brutally
Besieged within a huge impregnable wall
Whilst dispatching so niggardly untamed

Spendthrift consolation in abandoned
Squalor, shackled directly midstream
The staunchest memory is shriekingly bad
Diversely muddled in swarmy afterthought

Whilst excavating then relegating the dire
Dustbin of your life; stringent messengers
Protest the snatching transcriptions in the
Remonstrating promissory 'wandered thought

This emptied sensation keeps fruitlessly
Jabbering and glaringly elaborating wept
Gripping moments thus narrowly slipping into
A dark forced vacuum of permanent cul de sac

ENGORGING INSANITY

A woman like you is hard to find
But life has treated me kind
It's you that I wish to bind
And our passionate love entwine!

If we can try to apply then we can
Increase our supply and reach for
The sky; into the memories of
Yesteryear I do dwell, where

Our impacting love grew so swell
Our similarities just didn't gell
It's not as easy as to kiss n 'tell
Can we ever ring the church's bell?

What construed was delirious abnormality
There was no stability beyond immorality
My senses were submerged in fluffy vanity
Dubbed in a cluster of engorging insanity

ETCHING MY BRAIN

Where's the tranquility of fluffy
Nimbus clouds 'thunderbolt skies
It must be a mixture of you and
I Jointly relaxing in a passionate lie

You're healing hands 'sensual touch
Delivers unto me; much too much
I love the way it looks and feels
Etching my brain scratching my heels

The combustible energy of when love kneels
Many times I've had to pitter patter
Upon the slippery ebony slatter, we cannot
Afford to get any fatter, even if we

Eat the fish 'chips cholesterol batter
I want my stomach to look much flatter
So what's the matter? Doesn't life
Always reward you on a silver platter?

EXACERBATING TENSION

There's an exacerbating tension squeezing our esoteric love
Cunningly advancing towards us at a choky pallbearer's pace
Cloyingly smirking and annoyingly tolling the funeral bells
Consummately exhuming your fortune and to sit in your space

Your like an ageing prince clinging to almighty power
But your empire is crumbling like a withering flower
Periodically you tempt the saint to become a sinner
Yet in reality he will never be a righteous winner

FETISHNESS

It's SO comparitively strange to be clinging
To you'renon conformist intellectual values
Not nonpussed at the unsufferable burnishing
From an unexpected moral boosting furnishing

You're startlingly antagonistic n'rapturously
Pessimistic; curled in an active rendition of
Fetishness, thus wobbling banal replenishness
Smidgedly thrashing from the gritt de rigueur

As a symbol of suppression 'vile aggression
Wholeheartedly you break the chains from the
Socialite brains, streamlining valuable remains
How can we flush out, all of the sewage drains?

FIENDISH STUPOR

As the red dust settles etching upon your
Defeatist tune, an incredulous innovation
Impedes the stark adjectives of nostalgia
Sush parochial dieback accompanied aplomb

What a salubrious spectacle in the morbidly
Farcical shuffle of hybrid form; inhumanely
Torn, an unnerving explosion of cyclonic wit
A fiendish stupor trapped in a cancerous pit

Mysteriously snuffles whilst virulently catching
Then resisting the temptation of undue adulation
From the spotlight of your bloodied focusing eye
Modifying and intensifying, triumphantly purging

I drowsily drink your venom, from the sparingly
Cantharus cup, as the airstream of ill dealings
Accure in unexamined atavistic thought; harshly
Condemned are puissantly tamed abortive desires

Obsequious are the self contained acclimatizing
Fires; absorptively intervening, providentially
In the redistribution of many unpunished crimes
Imaginatively befriending the calculating minds

FLAP YOUR WINGS

Every time I look at youI freeze
And I wonder why you gently tease
Is this a game? Tell me please!
Next to fame you roll with ease

Have we lost what we first found
As I saturate this desolate town
For a fact that's pretty profound
On the rebound i thirst and hound

For a love that's not arid bound
What sort of a situation is this
MayI seal it with a loving kiss
Don't run away, from sweet bliss

Irresistably cultivating pleasant
Memmories, commemorating melodies
Why sizzle n'fry just flap your wings
And fly, my beautiful lady, butterfly

FUZZY MELANCHOLY

Have you seen an eagle fly, without wings
Or a dolphin swim in the sea without fins
Before I was blind, but now I can see
The radiant love that's dormant in me

I'm leaving the past far behind
As it stifled my blackened mind
With fuzzy melancholy so unkind
Sulphur was poured down my vine

I'm open minded to see
That temptation calls on me
How close can I ask to be? When
Serenity ploughs it's sprouting tree

Lies and deceit I'll toss away
Only truth can bestow and stay
All the fakeness must fade astray
And we shall have the minion play

GARBLE

What provision seals your decision
Why be so defensive when you're so
Comprehensive 'business extensive
Don't drive a barbecue stake in my

Brain then make me go insane
Let's stop pretending in bed
And look to whatever ahead
Where shall we draw the line

If I can't honestly have you as mine
The river moans; like a hungry beast
But you're invited to the royal feast
Must we garble, before we're deceased

GLOATED BREATHS

I closely listen to the gloated breaths
And witness many strange untimely deaths
We have a smorgasbord of ideas and such
Unobtainable desires inspired like fires

You keep importunately imposing your strict will
Like some exotic manifest aphrodisic strong pill
I feel so awkwardly insecure, because nothing is pure
I'm full of rage so T'll break the bars from the cage

There's not any form of aberration or much exploitation
But we 've wasted opportunities then sunk into damnation
What an idiotic mistake; should we be burnt at the stake?
We need an endless supply of comforting solitude and cake

GURGLING DELICACIES

When a modicum of thought cryptly tirades
The sardonic tale of hatching much deeper
Discontents 'toilet trained mind numbing
Menaces, mournfully unflustered us within

Gurgling rich delicacies prospering with
A clipboard condescension; attending the
Stalwart turbulence of modern technotalking
The enamoured companionship brought forward

By a fancy looking manicured brunette
Who knows, she may be the teacher's pet
The headmaster maintains a certain grading, while
Our roughneck coach, keeps us handsomely parading

HARMONIZINGLY SHAREABLE

I'm driving fast around the hairpin bends
And this road seems to have no clear ends
I don't envisage myself as been imperishable
I only see myself as harmonizingly shareable

The glacial waters illuminate the pristine scenery
Looking up at the tumultous, tumbling rocky cliffs
My life feels like it had it's fair share of biffs
Precipitously spanking me with itchy leather whips

What components are mostly found, in all living matter
When your life keeps moving 'your reserves do scatter
It's terribly horrible correcting the impoverishedly displaced
Don't you think it's time to look for a new compassionate mate

HEARTS FOR LOVE

I was a man of indecision and hate
Glorifying a miserable comfy state
Running needless without a soul to care
Something propelled me to a higher fare

I remember as children we played
Sheltered our fragile ego's away
We were so warmly naive and ready
To truly give our hearts for love

We have to search 'please ourselves
Cause were never content with enough
There is no other treasure like love
The ultimate pleasure is making love

What else comes for free from above
We can soar n'fly like a white dove
It's a feeling too good to give up
We must embrace it, and not let up

I remember as children we played
Sheltering our fragile ego's away
We were so warmly happy and naive
To truly give our hearts for love

HIT MY ZONE

You look like an atomic bomb has dropped on
Your face it's probably because you've been
Working in the wrong place, so I'll get off
Your case, but I won't give up on the chase

If you don't stop sobbing your crap
I might just shut your flaming trap
IfI see you all alone I will love you
To the bone because you've hit my zone

I don'+ seek to spoil or hard boil
I just want to wrap you in my foil
We'll have a coil and forget the toil
A car needs it's oil and flowers soil

IMPARLIO

If I had to lie
If I had to sigh
Would you be with me
Always in verse n'stride

You can't fib at me or
Look at me in the eye
So you tell me a quick lie
From your postgraduate tie

Don't terrorize then glamorize your stifling
Screeching sore eyes just happily harmonize
Why hide behind an assortment of caligo cries
That don "t add up to more than fruitless lies

Now let's make it abundantly clear
Before you and me vanish with fear
We should rekindle our loving scenario
While celebrating our wedding imparlio

INCREDIBLY DENSE

I want you to be snug n'happy as I
Change your nappy you 're the tonic
That's supersonic and our love has
Grown to more than merely platonic

I kiss your lips which is pure atomic an
I sense my good deed is done; for you my
Pretty little angelic number one. Have you
Committed an offence as you plead defence?

You're not that witty or incredibly dense even
If you fall off the fence. Do you want to pump
More weights or mess around with you're mates?
So why pay the bond then undetainably abscond?

INCURABLE AIL

Winners aren't afraid to lose even if they have unjust views
Like a jogger running in vain we must pass the point of pain
Some people are scared of fame, but to me it's a silly game
Inevitably aghast with tolling affairs 'unsuitable despair

Racked up with inconsistant pleasures chagrin measures
In a morphic vacuum without a suitable spirit of place
You may try to conceal the hefty vile mordacious space
Before we innocently get swept away in a frenetic pace

What epitaph do you expect me to unfold 'tenaciously hold
The incurable ail may set forth on a new trailblazing sail
Your multivalent approach softly commingles in a steady float
We have to stay afloat 'not fall victim to the pirate's boat

INDECOROUS MARK

Once I thought; that I'd never get over you
But that notion didn't hold completely true
I was so impressed and highly repressed that
I felt extremely flabbergasted n'sandblasted

My heart always had a soft spot for cute lovable you
Your charmingly attractive slim liposuctioned thighs
Airbrush lies 'intolerable alibi's were no surprise
Such a universal style in a slight incredulous smile

You made your naughty indecorous mark, right after dark
Blindly I tripped into the duck filled pond in the park
I felt like I was systematically laundered into Noah's Ark
I was struck by love's arrow 'knocked down like a sparrow

INFECTING FESTER

You say you wouldn't spit
Even if I on me was on stark flaming fire
But you forget that I 'm the one
That used to light up you're desire

I've courted you like a sly court jester
Protecting you from the infecting fester
Soothingly massaging you in a hot bubble bath
Sweetly serenading you from a candle lit path

The daffodils rise up so pretty as you suddenly cower
They love the freshness of the twilight summer shower
I listen to the tinkling of the masts and the lakewater lapping
at the
Jetty fast, I heed the nip in the air I look back but you're not
there

INNER CRAVING

I'm charmingly charismatic n'sposmatic
I'm melodramatic n'incredibly dogmatic
I love to drink straight qinn'tonic
And always try to fly so super sonic

I'm colorfully imaginative n'stimulative
I prefer no artificial preservative or
Superficial colouring 'additive; or some
Medically proven pain killing sedative

You instill a gut wrenching inner craving
To conceive a sought out original thought
You can visualize internalize then realise
And achieve a much fulfilling desired goal

I can run the golden mile and wink with style
I can meticulously educate 'elevate you're child
I'm not a mediocre teacher or a God fearing preacher
I can soothe your aching bones without the use of clones

ITCHY BRUISES

While skilfully snapping my itchy
Shrub scratched arms remembered
The almost crippling tumble which
Rendered me lame, for the rest of

My holiday, I was bristling in
Agonizing pain and clutching to
The serenity of our little girl
Trying to comfort her bruised up

Father! What bittersweet emotions
Her tender softly white skin trying
To clean away my growing black n'blue
Itchy bruises How will that confuse us?

LIVING IN A DREAM

Can you see these eyes? They're blue
Do you feel this heart? It loves you
When I'm with you I pleasantly unwind
I unleash feelings so heavenly divine

Do you think of me in your bed
Do you feel sad or pretty glad
Living in a dream, where have I been
You're such a candidly smooth talker

You can virtually do anything n'everything
Singing the right song, you can't go wrong
There is no solace for my constant burning
Baby for you, I am wholeheartedly yearning

LOVE IS FREE

I can still shed a silent lonely happy tear
To lift you much higher in the stratosphere
In this busy world are we that blind to see
You were made for me; and that love is free

When cool water evaporates from our sunny oasis
Affection filters through, the unpatchable leek
Romantic tales need to have a very happy ending
With love ascending and our hearts transcending

LOVESICK LIES

I sense the sadness unto you're eyes
Spitting many lonesome lovesick lies
There must be a storm, brewing in my
Teacup and a blizzard in a buttercup

The seasons changed and so did I
I tried to reflect and answer why
It's such a comical feeling when my
Brain does sing, I feel like a king

It's funny when you look at me strange
Perplexingly taut 'sigh, I can change
My sad song and confusingly wonder why
The love that I had left, so now I cry

I don't seek to open up old menacing wounds
I just wish to heat all of our embracing hoofs
Carefully ranging from you'reself centred cocoon
Gently yet firmly, in n'out of the womb, to the tomb

LULLABY VOICE

Diurnal images keep lodging quiescently in my quickle mind
Navigating from the dullish varying humdrum of the outside
Our garden flowers nature up as the spudded camelia's which
Are highlighted in the rosy sprinkling cup; you're milkwood

Shiny skin intermingles with your deceptive decolonizing eyes
You're stance is strangely still covered in a patchwork quill
I'm positive that I've made the right choice! As you keep on
Renumerating me with your silky, syllabicating lullaby voice

My mirror reflects the rays from your potash face exemplifying your
Lovely grace, there's not many people who can make me feel
   this way
And my vocabulary earnestly runs out of words for me to use
   and say
What else can T do to sweep you off your feet and to love you sweet

MEMORABLE SURPRISE

The tree without a root is akin to a
Fiddler without a flute sharp n'cute
Do you believe in astral travel? Or do you
Dabble in a mixture of metaphysical rabble

No one can really fly away; so they say
But we all wish to relive a notable day
Just like the time when you hugged me dearly
And whisked me warmly n "conversably far away

In the autumn park after dark, the hairy
Mangy growling dog did so chiringly bark
As I correctively pulled his muzzle seethe
Only to reveal it's crankily rotting teeth

Underneath the poplar tree I quickly nimble on
French fries, recollecting your flowering kiss
With creamy bliss, the world only offered lies
But we all wish to relive a memorable surprise

MENTAL FLAB

If your going to live, in the future
Then you must plan for you're future
If you don't have a goal you may lose your soul
And you might as well be Off the electoral roll

If you strive for nothing then you'll receive nothing
You must paint your fantasies sublime in marking time
Why suffer from mental flab look at Einstein and grab
All of the entrepreneurs had a vision and took a stab

Don't see a set back as a step back
It should make you defencibly aware
To better handle yourself with care
Unashamedly you could honestly dare

Don't let anyone make you think that
There's something you cannot do, because
You can do anything that you desire to do
That's so commonly true, so please do!

MOTHER WON'T YOU TELL ME

Mother won't you tell me
Oh father please let me know
I've been here for such a long time
An what have I got to honestly show

I'm trouble bound as I'm travelling around
I watch the stars as they plunge deep down
My ears are tuned to the forest fresh sound
Of a hundred raging horses galloping ground

Why can't you be all there is to be
Why can 't you see all there is to see
Why won 1 t you properly enlighten me
Why won't you listen to my daunt plea

Teacher won't you genuinely show me
How pleasant life is supposed to be
That I can live so happy 'fancy free
In a world where I am not meant to be

I've learned to shed my frustrating pain
With all the notions that are void in me
I've reached outside of my twisted shell
An the trouble that's been compacting me

Mother won't you tell me
Oh father please let me know
I've been here for such a long time
An what have I got to honestly show

MURMUR IN MY HEART

The darkness falls over our cosy tiny
Mudbrick cottage as the hungry wolves
Howl menacingly into the blistery wind
Moonlight pierces the night shining so

Bright onto your skintight, velvety dress
Casting it's shadow of mystery, festering
In the rainy autumn breeze, luxuriating the
Revengeful wrath that you zealously entwine

There's a blitzing murmur in my heart
As I wander about in the numbing dark
I can't go back to where I've been
For many torn horizons I have seen

The loneliness which I suffer, is not serene
A welcoming consolation is emphatically keen
I try to rekindle your joyous worldly charms
And still hold you in my embracing open arms

I dare to pistol whip then lick your delicate palms; as I
Notice the blackening purple bruises on your bulging arms
You're blood filled veins keep rattling like heavy chains
Can you seriously compete? In the shabby ditchwater games

NEVER MIND MY
BLEEDING MIND

In another time n'placei felt the
Happy memory which I trace no more
A stone broke the surface of the pond
It brought ripples of tears to my lame
Lonely hurting heart one more sad time

Never mind my bleeding mind
For I learnt from your disguise
In a fantasy world which rhymes
Were we not meant for eachother?
At least for a dimension in time

NO SECOND CHANCE

Vestiges of ghost towns are a flicker away
The rustling of eagle wings dither my stay
Repositories of bezants with solid escarpments
Arouse my curiosity to geological compartments

Your face is wrinkling 'accumulating mud dirt
From sadly swaddling cries, an inner mirky fog
Mirrors a cold resemblance of bittersweet lies
I don't live in a decorated ivory tower with a

Merry go round flower. I'd rather hide my shame
In the attic away than cower in a summer shower
If you lack the proper reinforcements you might
Make a foolhearty advance with no second chance

PACIFIC VELOCITY

I wish to lye on top of the docile ocean waves
And feel the pacific velocity of massaging rip
Our time and life slips beyond electrophoresis
From a groundswell cluster of shattered dreams

Luxuriantly chicaning a querulous muted note
Sandbaking you're chafing ego n'heedful mind
We cannot pretend to fathom the misery end
Even though I'm riding on a humpback trend

Scooting in the gloaming reclining sea from A to Z
The watershed is rapidly declining, but not for me
Our auspicous shadows pivot so tired and lonely
I will keep a light on in the dark for you only

PANDERING QUOTABILITIES

Why scrutinize and analyze the obnoxious portal
Barrage of uncontrollable dimwitted empty lives
Pandering quotabilities, by haggardly thronged
Misconceptions balkingly repatriating headlong

Exploitatively fricative 'solely vindictive are the
Old skinflint franchises; piddling grimaces from toy
Aspirantly asinine infidels. Irredeemably clustering
Unsplintering deceitful is the wrath of ascetic life

Counterparting some peristyle laudatory incongruity
Clangouring from a purging desultory into embryonic
Uproots; intrinsically straitlaced bedecked beyond a
Future timeslot, fashionably rife for abhorent fight

PANGS OF INDIGNITY

This God forsaken off the trail place
Reminds me of a 19th century colonial
Southern town where floorboards creak
And the lonely, haunting ghosts creep

Then I kick off the dripping mud from
My aching feet and shake the dust from
My silver string rotating cowboy kleats
You look like a beat up alley cat that's

Just wet it's tail from the approaching qale
My courage is ever dependable an my fortitude
Is highly commendable but our lives are merely
Expendable; as we fade into nothingness quietly

I disappear then re appear, like a former shadow
Of the many warrior's that I have fought and the
Loveliest valour which I have so rightfully sought
Whilst I cruise on this refugee Indian reservation

It's evidently clear that they now suffer from tiff
Pangs of indignity injustice 'constant depravation
They're once proud gleaming warrior nation has lost
Any form of it's firm affirmation with no salvation

PARRYING STARE

Sitting on the edge of oblivion
I stroll like a dying amphibian
My heart is broken beyond repair
As I inhale the dismissive stare

Undeniably accurate is you're duty of care
An I'd still like to taste you medium rare
Intensely congregating in illustrious flare
Expatiating foolishly with a parrying stare

The vengeance which I overwhelmingly feel
Is rebarbatively fierce to try to conceal
The parchment of our resolvable stature
Prolongs a feeling to sternly recapture

Like something that has been lost by years of
Neglect; which I meagerly choose to recollect
You and me earnestly try in vain to reconnect
It's really not up to us, to choose or select

PATCHAREE

I adore you're long straight jet black hair
It wallows so wild in the wind without care
Your intrinsic stare opens my heart so bare
I swear to always be honest and nice to you

In spirit and whatever you may decide to do
I know I can amuse 'ignite your inner fuse
But your mind wonders so painfully confused
We've gone past thick trials 'tribulations

It's been a very long fight for you to be free
And now you can smile and plant firm your tree
You remain so pure and simply pretty to me, just
Like a dangling bumble bee progressive Patcharee

PEACEFUL RUSTLE

Like watercoloured paintings freshly exhibiting
Silhouette mountains covered in layers of green
Neutralizing the incoercibly calming ambience
Incipiently coagulated n'inchoately thrusting

You are the blue sky and the bright sun
You always made me feel like number one
You rescued me from dullness n'depression
And gave me a solid positive consultation

You're the peaceful rustle between autumn leaves
You're the incessant coolness of summer's breese
You're the tingling wave that clings to the sand
You're the affectionate king that quides my hand

PEOPLE NEED TO BE SERVICED

Every suit needs it's tailor
An every sea has it's sailor
Every season has it's weather
You smile soft like a feather

How can an apple taste the same as
An orange, an apricot, or a banana
How can a torana drive the same as
A brand new hotted up turbo monara

How can a Gibson sound similar
To a Paul Reed Smith or Fender
People need to be serviced regularly
Just like cars, and electric guitars

Every waiter serves some qood tables
As an auto electrician replaces worn
Out cables; Would you prefer to clean
Out smelly stables or majestic gables

It's so hard trying to be in love with you
When you're heart isn't optimistically true
You can't mix oil with water and expect to drive
You can't drink arsenic instead of cola n'survive

PIRAHNA BANANA

I slept empty in my bed
A miserable tear I did shed
Why try to paint a loveless story
There's nothing left but vain glory

Do you still eat dry sour fruit
Or encourage you're new recruit
Just bite like a savage pirahna
Then have another fruity banana

It is better to build a relationship
On love 'trust instead of lies n'lust
I don't belong in a prehistoric cave
So let's forget to rave 'start to save

Don't let my age fool you
Because I still can cool you
Why arque with fear then disappear
Our love is like a spontaneous cheer

Is that abundantly clear, my dear
We've been here for only a short while
And you're displaying aristocratic style
You manage to make everything worthwhile

Put on your cape then change the tape
Tomorrow is a brand new sunny day
That's why I will play in a funny way
The night is young so let's have some fun

PLACID GAME

I'm not sore, I'm just aiming to score
Tim not clever I just want you forever
If I sit in your class will you kick my ass
You say I'm the best but I have to pass the test

From the top of my head to the tip of your toe
You keep me running so I'm not awfully slow
Gathering stormclouds eventually collide
Causing us to bitterly shiver and cry

Cool clear dreams lessen my violent screams
Sugarland flavours of sights that I've seen
Meticulously decorated in opulent green
The infinite arrow is bellowing obscene

Regurgitating amongst giddy withering shame
Please reassure me that it 's never the same
In n'out of this tumultously awesome placid game
What determining factor can we peremptorily gain

POWER TRIP

Are you going to bring me breakfast
On a tray, or try to lead me astray
You're all revved up 'ready to go
And no one else can steal the show

I'm not capable to swing and groove
But I'll play it, delicately smooth
I feel the punch protruding me rude
What's for lunch, my attentive dude

We are living from day to day
But finding love is so far away
I can see the look in your eyes
Because the camera never lies

This may not sound like a true story
But I still can steal you're glory
I'm looking thru a tear, because
I can always cherish you dear

Your the captain steering the ship
As you shoot straight from the hip
Riding out on the imagination strip
Did you sell out on your power trip

PRISM BIND

Why don't you open up your heart
And let the fury gently depart
The way you lock your door makes
Me yearn for you, so much more

All the delicate subtleties you implore
It's zig zag to your door and nig nag
To your store; skateboard off the floor
Why get steamed up over a cold shower

Your daffodils grow so pretty as you cower
Amongst the freshness of a summer's shower
Will you subpoena yourself or resort to
An erratic separatism of the prism bind

What excites your curiosity? Is it pure
Ferocity or a collaborative generosity?
I'm aware that you wont advocate any leniency
On what constellation do you find expediency?

PRUDENT PROVISO

The wheels of fortune, increases commercial
Activity; revenue and profit on many floors
It's not that easy to forecast or precisely
Estimate the initial production line chores

There's a yardstick to be stroked repeatedly
For every successful core, there has to be a
Companion notebook for each department store
The pie-chart and linear graphs truly reveal

The highlight scores; your consortium is enamoured with
A precious piggy bank amount, from a stock market count
What a coordinated manipulative, stepping stone account
The work edict is reflectively amiable 'hyper asthenic

Equipped with compact skills and no commando thrills
You ambush and flush out the weak! There's a certain
Anomaly within the meek, with your high fashion attire
And lips on fire, you transpose the rich from the geek

The retinue in your unofficial satchel is rookie material
Thus enhancing the audience by purchasing monetarily neat
Such an enormous feat! The prudent proviso is a master deviso
Dehorting the all too cheap; maybe it's time for you to sleep

RECKLESS INSTABILITY

Riding above the snowcapped wintery peak
Miles away from the arable, shrubby heap
I'm unimpeded by rising torrential rain
Or sandstorms cane; acutely I'm in pain

The chipped flint spearpoint is notched
Between my chest, muttering with detest
We cannot abrade the pessimistic activism or
Hitherto schism so let's use professionalism

What aegis is there against the agistedmultitude
Of perspicaciously construed, heavy enemy bombing
Do you think you'll ever stop you 're silly sobbing
why don't you go away and do some bargain shopping

Is there any mobility beneath your reckless instability?
How can we psychoanalyze, you're compelling inabilities?
My only thought was of you, qiving me love like I never knew
Transfixing the insequential periods, with realistic myriads

RENDER INSANE

Our emotions were repercolating fresh in our minds
Grudgingly brutish was the unenviable incursion of
The reascending disqualifying sickly abusive times
Manly washed away in a mud racked terrential flood

The constant variable lies collectively transit in
Your insomnic brain, posing a mental drain to your
Crucial vein catapulting yourself to render insane
Chronicling the intervention for a revisionist set

I was so overwhelmed, with grief in my heart because
Our love did not last; like a colourful patchwork of
Thinning paint, in hindsight you made me feel like a
Saint! Some dazzling sparks lit the fuse in my heart

Exploding in a joyous start without betrayal I was on a
New rail thunderously escaping the clutches of old yale
Even though I felt quite frail, Iperservered through the
Savagely blinding unrelentless hail; easily I did prevail

RISIBLE GESTURES

I extil my agony with angry swollen tears
Then die a death which no one sadly hears
Unpure textures, mixing the thalamus bind
Risible gestures risk above resolute rind

Subtle pleasures frisk my sherbet mind
I'm not rude, I'm just crude, and I'll
Hope you won "t mind, when I do intrude
You're benighted, inanimate, interlude

From reality I've strayed 'flapped my stealv
Wings along the bay, dimming the ultra violet
Ray; you're schizophrenic mind is skyward bound
Your blabbing heart cruises the millenial round

RUPTURING MIND

In another time 'place I tried to
Envisage the love I could not cage
A falling boulder broke the surface of
The pond which dimpled pleasantly fond

Superlatively I could not escape the bond
The greenish wet reeds were worn and long
Grossly goosebumping my soul, in a swirling
Drowning violent epitah of a crippling cold

Never you mind my delicately rupturing mind
For I painfully endured your pestering bind
In all those obscure years that you were mine
Never did I seek to drink from another's wine

SELDOM SLIP

I'm crying from the creepy grave
But I'm still trying to be brave
Even though I'm six feet under
It won't stop my reign of plunder
It's like a clap of mighty thunder
A legacy that's filled with wonder
The sandy pebbly subtropical shallow
Lagoon is where I'll be heading soon
I'm respectfully symbolized yet often
Offensively and needlessly criticised
My sticky fingers will do the trick
And prevent you from getting sick
It's not all about being super slick
It's watching out where you seldom slip
I'm tired of going on another business trip
What I need now, is to settle down; quick!

SEVERED PAW

If we could only employ a compass quide, then
Happiness cannot be impossible for us to find
Whilst deep inside we often dread to outwardly
Struggle but I want you to stay out of trouble

You threw yourself flouncingly in my face
But I ran so much faster and won the race
You pushed me into the hungry wolf's jaws
As he freezingly shunted, blindly howling

With a severed paw drooling forever sore
Your like a fussy artist trying to paint
A masterpiece picture on a canvass sheet
Squirting a kaleidoscope of colors neat

Wiping away the dirt with the floorcloth
I totally cherish everything that you do
And I know I cannot give enough to you
So my love for you must really be true

SIBLINGS OF YESTERYEAR

Thinking back to a smoother time and place
I cherish the memory which grace no more
Gunfire breaks the serene echoes in my mind
Thus thwarting the cool clear waters of our

Radiant love which certainly was a glorious
Gift from up above! So why chastise my soul
For an unplausible ruminating unattainable
Goal? Why do we liquidate our future bowl?

Never in my life did I think I'd get it right
Now I'm teething at all the prevailing strife
Luminating between the war torn courage we
Place into gear; as siblings of yesteryear

SINEW SWOLLEN CHILD

Jot down all the entombed deleterious mustiness
My incomprehensible asinine sinew swollen child
Nibbling at life within a short circumference mile
Ebbed in debt, veering off vedette, temerity's pet

Contagious is your bet in the sharp etched set
Pertinently perturbing in a vacuum of neon jet
Cushioning delegates of a turbulent indispensible
Net; irreparable bow-leggedness, warrants you yet

Rigid compunctions nullify you're spontaneous id
Nevertheless, you learn faster than a docile kid
Irredeemably responding to doubt, in silence sit
Whatever the world offers, you assurgently befit

SLAGHEAP OF INDECISION

I wasn't offered a seat so that's why
I still stand upright on my flat feet
In this roomful of mirrorsI juggernaut
At the rosy carnival of life, n'flutter

Garishly is the creation; moaning like a
Strange mutation devoid of all sensation
Does camaraderie come armed, with some new
Repellant? Unmarked so permanently gallant

Distractedly cloistered among division
Slumping on the slagheap of indecision
What vision does exist in mass revision
Brooding with you're prejudice decision

SQUANDERING CULPRIT

Your face is hard like mountain ash
Boy it must have taken quite a bash
You must have given up smoking hash
Your eyes ravage like a savage fire

You stroll around in glamorous new attire
Wreaking havoc on the tree feller's spire
As you spiridly precipitate a congenital vote
Shelving the past with some emboldening quote

You can turn the darkest night into clearest day
You can huddle me into frantic orgasmic foreplay
You can clean out, every once common dirty disease
With slender ease, as I jubilantly yell yes please

Your a diminutive resident sourpuss, drunk, sodden and fed
A consummate philanderer in a chanteuze bed! A squandering
Culprit in a stranglehold shed, outmuscling the competition
Till they 're dead, the pressure cooker has explodingly bled

STERN DELIBERATION

I want to see the sun set in your eyes
And the moon ricochet, above the skies
Soon I'll avoid all my nasty ego ticks
Then I'll feel, like I've had my kicks

There's nothing more than I totally desire
My fondness for you, rages like a wildfire
Because you're the woman, that can set me on fire
I wish to aspire and perspire to something higher

As I slip into the exclusive designer label attire
The wheels of motion have been pumped on each tyre
Seldom do sense the lovely pleasure to marvel at
Such feminine treasure, wholeheartedly I do extend

My warmest gratitude at your level headed sensible
Attitude, lovingly I seek to appreciatively please
You're such a genuine inspiration offering stern
Deliberation with true spectacular intrepidation

Your intelligence astounds me as your eloquence
Surrounds the logic you possesprofounds me
Your cool calm collective approach is above reproach
I'm the selective pupil and your the uplifting coach

SWAYING PALMS

I'm bathing in the lusciously warm
Tropical sunshine whilst embracing
The fragrantly mystical colours, as calm
Gentle breezes filter thru swaying palms

Dazzling they're lofty colorful splendour
Cooling the ambient summery sticky hot air
I'm relaxingly snorkelling in balmy soft love
Trying to eclipse the humid sun; just for fun

It's halfway to heaven, and one step to paradise
It's the silly season where everything tastes nice
You're worries and fears seem to casually drift away
When a smart vibrant fresh new face circulates the day

TARNISHED YEARS

Angrily you vented your animalism into
My poor little frail, meandering heart
Then violently jolted onto the bedpost
Throwing the blankets and pillows away

Upwards from our sinful hotbed, our osmosis
Was like some overtly fluctuating psychosis
My body always yearns for what we previously had
As I remember the gracious time we shared in bed

Fiddling over you're slim sexually toned longlegs
Whilst rowing in the solitary sea your oleaginous
Scent is telepathically sent to me; the dailiness
Of life perpetuates the lustrum to relieve strife

A false pretence seems to stifle all of our gears
Eminently modifying our excitingly tarnished years
With the pre emptivegrimmace of sweaty clammy tears
We've grudgingly encamped by harassing breaching fears

THUNDERBOLTING SKIES

I have to test the hot boiling water with my
Innocent little toe, and open the windowsill
Of my belligerent mind thre the partial bind
Where's the tranquility of the fluffy clouds

And thunderbolting skies? It seems like a huge
Mixture of you and I, relaxing I in a lovely lie
I felt as though I've been brutally punched down
Into the entire earth lying in ashen nothingness

Our mangy provocative love was like a tittering dove
There lies a sordid silent testimony to your alimony
There 's a gusty open air backdrop, shuffling in you 're
Heart wrenching shop barbarously belting out it's chop

TILL WE WED

She tries to face the day
And thinks of words to say
Some lies are gone but stay
How thoughtful is love's way

When we run n'hide and play
We shouldn't intend to delay
The prosperity of being gay
There is a necessity to stay

In between the dawning day
Our dreams lay in our head
As we shed our love in bed
We must be careful till we wed

TIMID AURA

You tear my delicate linen sweaty shirt
With your venomous long clutching claws
They re not indolent little feline paws
Yet you wipe the vaseline jelly from my

Aching dry soreish sunburnt cracked lips
And you unzip my pants to run your cobra
Fingernails over my excitedly firm tits
As you tongue kiss my elated frosty nape

Biting my soul with so much sheer ecstacy
There's no other place that I'd rather be
Foreshadowing you're willowy frail frame
Hovering in a propagated, plethora flame

Like a bloodthirsty tarantula sucking me dry
The lysis of colonial indicativeness; we try
Encroaching upon my blood letting timid aura
While grouching down on my humble ego storer

TRIFLING HEART

Rainforests circulate water from tree to tree
But you're love for me, is nowhere to see
Your toothbrush is too big for your mouth
As we store old wine in a cosy new bottle

That's redundant of a fresh creamy throttle
Someone else always runs your slippery race
Wholeheartedly you deliver a screaming pace
I'm not a slick private investigator or any

Whizbang insurance estimator, you're not an
Art curator or a flash seafaring navigator
Don "t think SO contaminated or disanimated
The gates of love, should swing wide open

To avoid the nudging buckle chik of sheer
Heart attack; to something less exuberant
In acrid black, the key to love is set in
Stone, a trifling heart cannot postphone!

UNIVERSAL SPHERE

Life cannot get chillier so
I'm keen I've got you now at last,
But I need To recreate a better past; just listen
To the universal sphere, it's bringing

Us closer to a user friendly hemisphere
You say you never made it on your own
That's because you are a closet clone
You have to install new plaster just to

Cover up the latest, diabolical disaster
I walked no longer in disarray when love
Showed me a cuter way, my heart sparkled
So fresh n'gay I was happy come what may

UNWIND

The things that you say do
Don't reflect what you so
The lies that you spin
Don't hold to be true

How can you retrace
The stages in your life
And think of things unkind
Don't be sad, just unwind

And recollect the jovial happy times
When all the world did genuinely shine
You're like a child quivering on a cold dark night
Eagerly awaiting for something tasty to quickly bite

VAGRANTLY HARKING

Let's not start a new debate and end up
Arguing callously, with unrational hate
So why do you place me silently on hold
And get knocked out so ambiguously cold

Romantically you jump deep in the puddle
I'd like to give you a cute giant cuddle
You're superbly despatchable sequestered
Attitude displays delicate ramifications

It's the law of the land to pay you're
Tax on demand; stop your timid barking
Just pay for the cheap, hourly parking
As you're lust keeps vagrantly harking

VELUTINOUS ECLECTICISM

Your sharp scissored knife pierces my pale
Soft skin so ripe, without clear conscious
Unexcusably shameless; and undeniably cold
The diaspora are drift netting unannounced

Like a weeping lost child my capabilities are
Drowning in the unrequited sea, impermanently
Supplemented with a handicapped synthesis of
Velutinous eclecticism shrouded in mysticism

Strikingly enough there's an untitled tenant
Lieutenant; his manners collude the triptych
Pertinacious planners 'industrious spanners
Some implication of solicitude is maintained

You're long fingered infallible hand rests
Comfortably with an ignoble immiscible mind
Cogitating in a penurious frost hugging bind
Which scenario will you earnestly concubine?

WALLOWING VAPOURS

You're wallowing vapours are now embalmed
In my battle torn, bloody bequeathed skin
Unnerving the pandemonium of banishment
Within the incomparable unnigard malice

There's a unilateral legacy for equatorial formations
From the ice region glaciers to tropical destinations
You look like you've fallen into a dirty black trench
Your ineptitude has uncovered a crystalline old bench

The tornado is angrily whirling;shockingly twirling
Where moments away, from nature in impending whirring
A distinct luminous replica begins to vaguely appear
Pushing my spirit beyond the higher leviathan sphere

Mildly, there's a message yet not so clear
Can I swear an oath to keep you near?
I'll qive my life, for you my dear!
Is everything enough, or do you still fear?

WEEPING MEADOWS

I'm searching for the secrets in your head
I'm tussling with you in my king sized bed
You're lonely heart is desperately lunging
Out to me embellishing what love should be

You keep yourself stealthily at arms length
Nudging past the discrepancy of sheer doubt
Staving off the brutal torturous colossal bout
What else can I consistently sacrifice or qive

How long must I arquably suffer or predatory live
The shadows have fallen without an arguable sound
Like the soft crisp will O the wisp angelic round
Only to disappear into the weeping meadows ground

WHATEVER HAPPENED TO WOODSTOCK

I don't have much money
And I don't really care
To support a system that's
False and not totally fair

I'm going to turn my back on all
The lies and unrealistic expectations
Illusion's confusion's blocking out my brain
With some pent up heavy handed patronizing vile

Whatever happened to Woodstock?
Over half a million rolled up there
Chanting for freedom, peace and love
A nuclear free planet 'some clean fresh air

What we've got to do now
Is paint a brand new picture
Of love and sharing in order to
Abolish the clutches of poverty's snaring

Whatever happened to Woodstock?
Over half a million rolled up there
Chanting for freedom, peace and love
A nuclear free planet 'some clean fresh air

WHIRLPOOL IN YOUR PANTS

I don't seek to plagiarise your ideas
Or minimise your casual bohemian life
I won't wish to diffuse your angst
Or cause a whirlpool in your pants

Anyhow, we can crawl around like ants
I never got to kiss the sweetest lips
In town, because you were always too
Unique to consider and have me about

I may not be the greatest guy that has ever been
But you have never ever witnessed what I've seen
As I watch the three quarter moon turning full
I can imagine feeding you by the swimming pool

WE CAN ENJOY

I want to share my dreams
And ambitions with you
I want to share my fears
And frustrations with you

I wish to seek out all
My passions with you
I wish to seek out all
My fashions with you

We can enjoy, love making!
Just like hot bread baking
We can melt the arctic ice
With fire 'sizzling spice

We can have many little things
That are nice and will suffice
I'll cherish you till the day I die
But for now, it's time to say goodbye

WEEKEND LOVER

You were my folly
I was your fool
Tainted in love
I lost my cool

How could I believe
The trickery you spun
You smiled at me
It was such fun

The golden web of lies
Became undone
Wholeheartedly you've
Lost then won

I don't need to read
A bedtime story
Or listen to your
Fame n'glory

I don't want to be
Your weekend lover
And share you with
Some other

You won't need to
Sadly chase it
Whatever you do
Just face it

When you place your red
Lipstick onto my shirt
I'll put it on
But still I hurt

If you leave the towel
In the bubble bath
I'll pull it out
Then qive it a rub

The champagne no longer remains on ice
The caviar dips have lost their spice
Valentino and Chanel do not suffice
Do we really have to think twice?

WHAT'S LEFT FOR ME TO DO

I was thinking of things
To say to you
I was dreaming of things
That we could do

I devoted my whole life
Just for you
You cannot imagine
How fond I was of you

You blessed my soul as I never knew
I looked up with respect at you
I would have done anything, for you
How can I say the same is true?

You're love couldn't stick like glue
You packed up then left without a clue
Now I look but find there's nothing new
My behaviour has changed from hot to blue

So what's left for me to do?
I'll just pick up the pieces
Of my beqotten life then look
Forward to finding a new wife

WHAT S PREDICTED?

My grandmother clenched her wrinkling
Fists up in the sky then thrusted all
Venting emotion towards my body. why?
With a gnawing in my gut rumbling sly

She looked at me like an old dying wolf
That's moaning and howling through it's
Withering teeth, it needs to pass on years
Of wisdom to the other members in his pack

For all his life, he's been such a sad sack
Feeling the urgency to get his message thru
So we can all acquire a new point of view
Astoundingly, my grandmother said to me

I'VE LIVED THROUGH
WORLD WAR I AND II

So I've got more than just a savvy clue
Of what the next one will potentially do
Though I'm highly gifted I can't shake off

What's predicted?

WITHERING SHAME

We need to develop sound strong skills
Instead of half witted shallow thrills
Then boost up on our confidence pills
We need answers to work out questions

Don't sit in silence, without defiance
Explore the reliance to alter deniance
Whenever we obtain real evidence we gain
Knowledge then we shall eat our porridge

Why be a masterful liar n'aprisoner
Of desire? We keep regurgitating the
Flame, consisting Of withering shame
In essence what do you hope to gain?

WOODSMOKE

I liked you not that long ago
But you're love did not flow
So I stood stagnantly slow
With barely nothing to show

I had every reason to crow
As I missed your radiant glow
How can I ruthlessly overthrow
Every cynical spit that you throw

You're love was like woodsmoke
Blaring with a lamenting stroke
I started courting you with opening doors
But it dismally ended, in a caveat clause

YESTERDAY'S YAWNING

Your eyes do the glancing and my heart
Is happily dancing 'forever romancing
Your tight waistline stockings leave me
Squealing at my throat, that's why I am

So prudently careful not to miss the boat
Even if I drown with your love I'll float
I believe we should try some new stuff
To disintegrate the moulting fisticuff

I don't mind tangling with your love
But you leave me dangling with a hug
In the decomposing abattoirs of psyche
What we once loose is what we can find

Another relationship on ice sparkling
And spawning like a brand new morning
How can we capture tomorrow,'s dawning
In a world where yesterday 's yawning?